Contents and how to use them

Golden Time Activity List — If possible 'blow up' to A3 size and display in classroom. Children sign up each week. Popular activities need to go on a rota system 1

Warning Signs — Junior and Infant signs. These are placed next to the child as a visible warning. They can later be removed if the child responds to the warning.................................. 2

Loss of Golden Time Chart — When a child loses Golden time, please enter name in column and tick appropriate box. N.B. keep this document in a private place 3

Earning Back Golden Time Contract — Children are able to earn back Golden time they have lost by agreeing to work on a specified goal 4

Do Not Disturb Signs — Individual signs for children to display when they wish to work undisturbed. Put on card and fix a support to the back of it, so they can be stood up on table 5

Do not Disturb Circle Time Sign — Sign to display on classroom door during Circle Time........... 6

Golden Coins — Children are given a 'coin' for achievement in work or behaviour................................. 7

Special Award — when they have achieved a specified number of 'coins' they receive the accompanying award 8

Golden Eggs — Children are given an egg for achievement in work or behaviour.......................... 9

Special Award — wh... spe... th... ac...

Invitation to Circle Time — Invitations for children... give to others, e.g. special guest, parents, lunchtime supervisor to join in Circle Time with them 11

Lunchtime Congratulations — Commendation notes for lunchtime supervisors to give to children. Children hand these in to their class teacher and receive an agreed reward, privilege, sticker, etc. 12

Lunchtime Booklet — Notes are stapled into a booklet. Supervisor initially notes down a child s name on a warning pad. If the child does not heed the warning, he/she is given a page from the booklet with appropriate box ticked. This is handed to the class teacher who then withdraws privilege or carries out other agreed sanction 13

Special Table Invitation — Lunchtime supervisors have a special table with table cloth and/or vase of flowers, etc. and/or spring water. Each Friday they hand out invitations to some children who have kept the Golden Rules, inviting them to sit at this table the following week 14

Responsibility Chart — A list of responsibilities is drawn up during Circle Time. Each week teacher or children enter names. List is displayed in classroom 15

© Jenny Mosley Consultancies, 28A Gloucester Road, Trowbridge, Wiltshire BA14 0AA Tel: 01225 767157 Fax: 01225 755631 Website: www.circle-time.co.uk

Reminder Notes	For class teachers to hand out to children...................... 16	
Good Thinking	Commendation for good ideas, good concentration, etc. 17	
Encourager Notes -	Notes to be given out as encouragers for children trying to improve work or behaviour 18	
Thank You Letter	This can be used by the children to give to any adult, or vice-versa 19	
Kindness Leaves	Each child completes a printed statement or fills in a blank leaf. The leaves are coloured in and mounted on a wall display of a bare tree or stapled to a real branch .. 20	
Helping Hands	Children write in comments on cut-out hands. These are then coloured in and displayed as a frieze around the wall 21	
All About Me	These four pages focus on self assessment and affirmation 22-25	
Feelings Colour Chart	Each child has a chart to colour in the various feelings 26	
Flowers for our Classroom Garden	Each child is given a cut-out flower to colour in and stick a photo of their face in the centre. The flowers are displayed in 'our classroom garden' 27	
Balloon Chart	Each child is given a balloon chart to colour in and write something they like or are good at in each balloon 28	
Family Tree	Each child is given a family tree to colour in and stick on cut-out photographs of family and pets 29	
Individual Target Encouragers	Instructions for use 30	
	Selection of target sheets to encourage children to keep to their agreed targets of work or behaviour 31-39	
Target Diary	Daily target record for child and teacher's comments on progress made 41	
Tiny Achievable Tickable Target Chart	Target chart for use with 'children beyond'	
	Instructions 42	
	Charts 43	
Class Team Honours	This can be used to celebrate a child's success in becoming more integrated into the class 'team' or for any other achievement that brings benefit to the class 44	
Achievement Ladder	Especially useful as an 'encourager' for younger children to reach their target.	
	Instructions 45	
	Ladder 46	
	Figures for achievement ladder 47	
Achievement Record	Chart for teacher to keep a record of class progress 48	
Well Done Letter	Special letter from teacher to child for any extra curricular achievement, e.g. swimming, learning to ride bike, making a cake for mummy 49	
Top Secret Note	Teacher uses this note to commend any child who can't accept public praise. The teacher writes a message and leaves the note in the child's drawer. The child does not have to acknowledge receipt of it 50	
Golden Rules for Parents	A copy of the Class Golden Rules that can be sent home for parents to sign. 51	

© Jenny Mosley Consultancies, 28A Gloucester Road, Trowbridge, Wiltshire BA14 0AA Tel: 01225 767157 Fax: 01225 755631 Website: www.circle-time.co.uk

Golden Time Activity List

Activity	Bring in Educational Game	Computer	Visit Other Class	Extra Art			
Week							
Week							
Week							
Week							
Week							
Week							
Week							

WARNING

Name ....

WARNING

Name ....

Infant

WARNING

Name ....

WARNING

Name ....

Junior

Loss of Golden Time Chart

Name	5 mins	10 mins	15 mins	20 mins	25 mins	30 mins

For week ending ....

Earning back Golden Time Contract

I agree to ....

.... (target)

in order to earn back .... minutes of Golden Time.

Keep the Golden Rules

Signed .... pupil

Signed .... teacher

Earning back Golden Time Contract

I agree to ....

.... (target)

in order to earn back .... minutes of Golden Time.

Keep the Golden Rules

Signed .... pupil

Signed .... teacher

© Jenny Mosley Consultancies, 28A Gloucester Road, Trowbridge, Wiltshire BA14 0AA Tel: 01225 767157 Fax: 01225 755631 Website: www.circle-time.co.uk

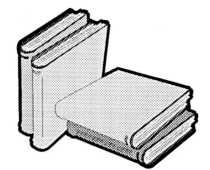

Do Not Disturb

I am working

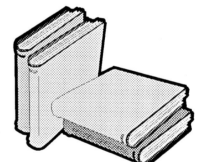

Do Not Disturb

I am working

5

Do Not Disturb

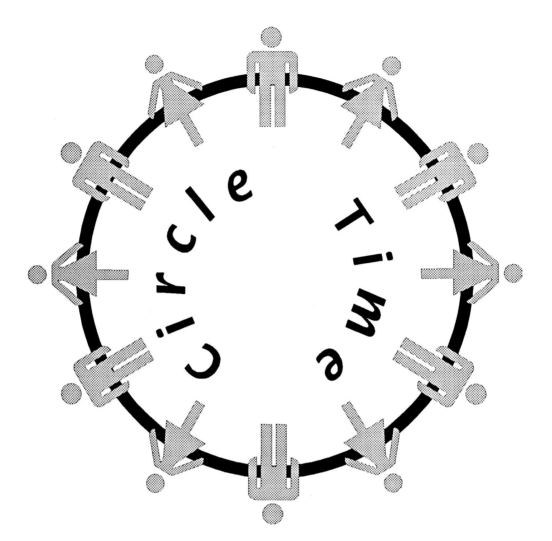

We are having

Circle Time

We are having

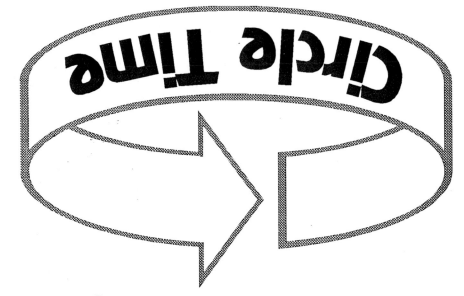

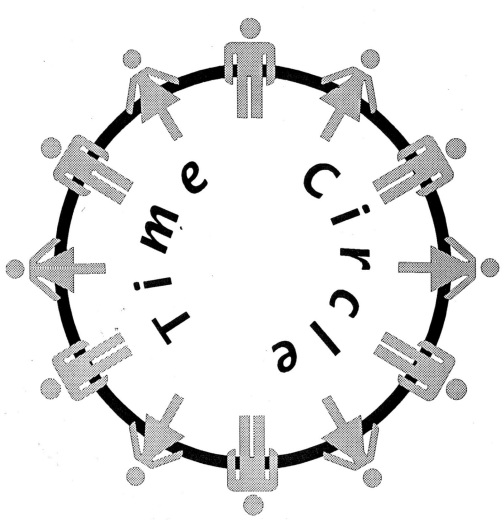

Do Not Disturb

Golden Coins

Special Award

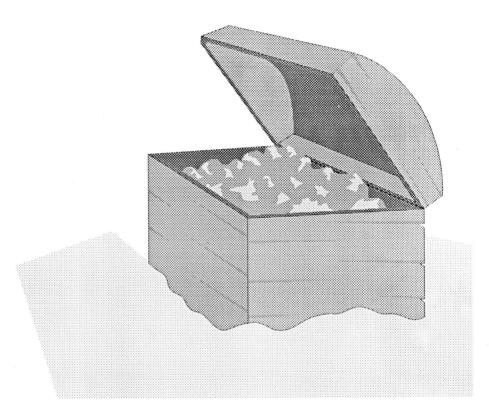

Well done ....

for earning ...... Golden Coins

Signed ....

Golden Eggs

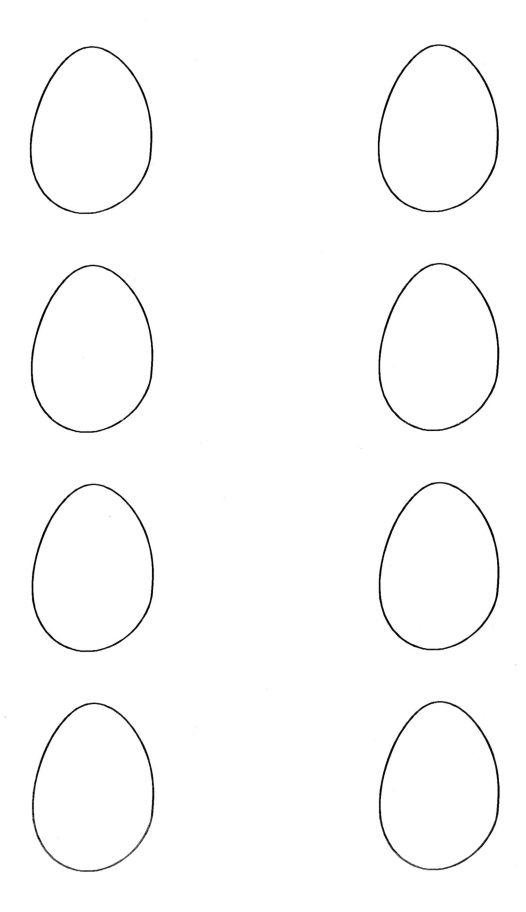

Special Award

Well done ....

for earning ...... Golden Eggs

Signed ....

Invitation
to Circle Time

Dear ....

We would like to invite you to
our Circle Time on .... (date)
at .... (time)

Invitation
to Circle Time

Dear ....

We would like to invite you to
our Circle Time on .... (date)
at .... (time)

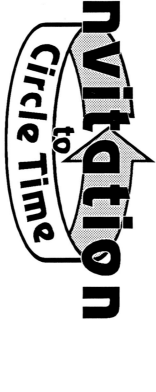

Invitation
to Circle Time

Dear ....

We would like to invite you to
our Circle Time on .... (date)
at .... (time)

Invitation
to Circle Time

Dear ....

We would like to invite you to
our Circle Time on .... (date)
at .... (time)

Lunchtime Congratulations

Name .... □ □ □ □ □

You were kind to others

You kept to the Golden Rules in the dining area

You played well with other children

You kept calm

You stood quietly and patiently in line

Signed.............................

Lunchtime Congratulations

Name .... □ □ □ □ □

You were kind to others

You kept to the Golden Rules in the dining area

You played well with other children

You kept calm

You stood quietly and patiently in line

Signed.............................

© Jenny Mosley Consultancies, 28A Gloucester Road, Trowbridge, Wiltshire BA14 0AA Tel: 01225 767157 Fax: 01225 755631 Website: www.circle-time.co.uk

Circle Time

We are having

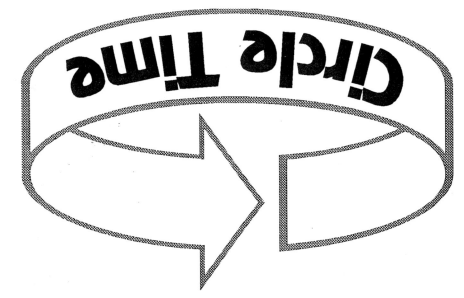

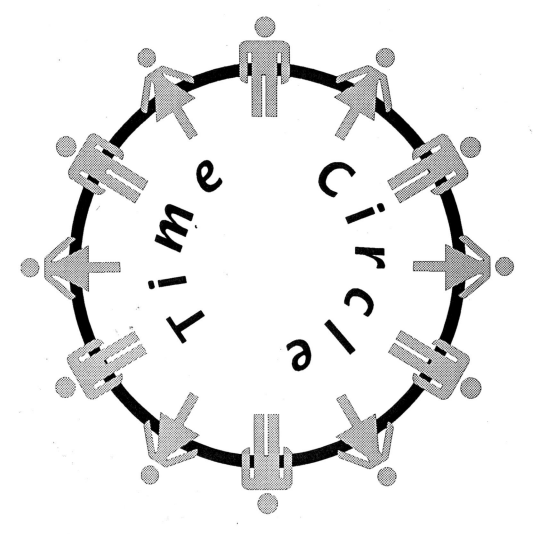

Do Not Disturb

Golden Coins

Special Award

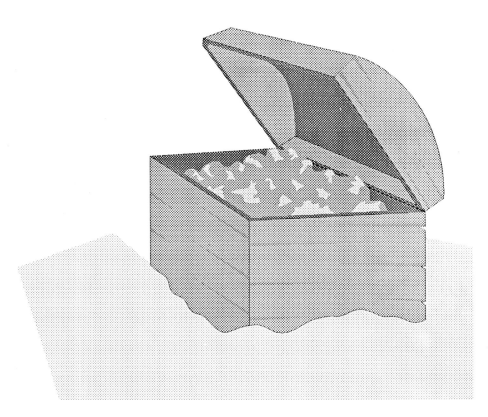

Well done ....

for earning ...... Golden Coins

Signed ....

Golden Eggs

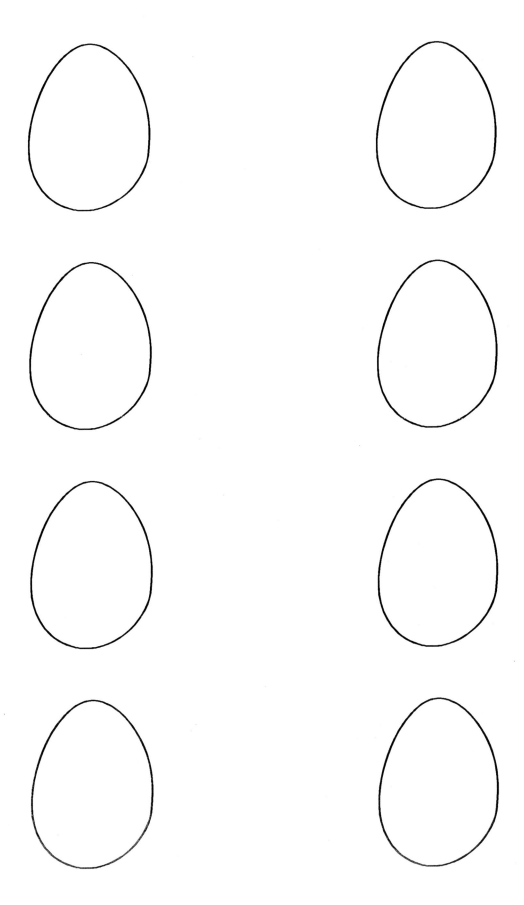

Special Award

Well done ....

for earning ...... **Golden Eggs**

Signed ....

Invitation
to
Circle Time

Dear ....

We would like to invite you to
our Circle Time on .... (date)

at .... (time)

Invitation
to
Circle Time

Dear ....

We would like to invite you to
our Circle Time on .... (date)

at .... (time)

Invitation
to
Circle Time

Dear ....

We would like to invite you to
our Circle Time on .... (date)

at .... (time)

Invitation
to
Circle Time

Dear ....

We would like to invite you to
our Circle Time on .... (date)

at .... (time)

Lunchtime Congratulations

Name ....

You were kind to others

You kept to the Golden Rules
in the dining area

You played well with other children

You kept calm

You stood quietly and patiently in line

Signed.................................

Lunchtime Congratulations

Name ....

You were kind to others

You kept to the Golden Rules
in the dining area

You played well with other children

You kept calm

You stood quietly and patiently in line

Signed.................................

Lunchtime Booklet

Name.........................

I am disappointed because:

You have deliberately
hurt another child ☐

You did not listen to me ☐

You hurt someone's feelings ☐

You broke the Golden Rules
in the dining hall ☐

You have broken the Golden
Rules in the playground ☐

Signed.........................
Lunchtime Supervisor

Lunchtime Booklet

Name.........................

I am disappointed because:

You have deliberately
hurt another child ☐

You did not listen to me ☐

You hurt someone's feelings ☐

You broke the Golden Rules
in the dining hall ☐

You have broken the Golden
Rules in the playground ☐

Signed.........................
Lunchtime Supervisor

Lunchtime Booklet

Name.........................

I am disappointed because:

You have deliberately
hurt another child ☐

You did not listen to me ☐

You hurt someone's feelings ☐

You broke the Golden Rules
in the dining hall ☐

You have broken the Golden
Rules in the playground ☐

Signed..........................
Lunchtime Supervisor

Lunchtime Booklet

Name.........................

I am disappointed because:

You have deliberately
hurt another child ☐

You did not listen to me ☐

You hurt someone's feelings ☐

You broke the Golden Rules
in the dining hall ☐

You have broken the Golden
Rules in the playground ☐

Signed.........................
Lunchtime Supervisor

Dear.....................

Because you have kept to the Golden Rules in the Dining Room, you are invited to sit at our special table next week.

signed.....................
Lunchtime Supervisor

Dear.....................

Because you have kept to the Golden Rules in the Dining Room, you are invited to sit at our special table next week.

signed.....................
Lunchtime Supervisor

Responsibility Chart

for week beginning...............

Responsibility	Name

Reminder

Name ....

Remember to ....

....

....

Signed ....

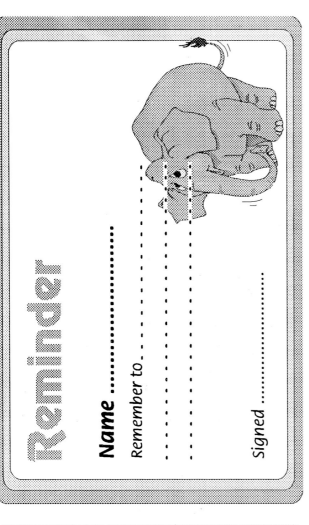

Reminder

Name ....

Remember to ....

....

....

Signed ....

Reminder

Name ....

Remember to ....

....

....

Signed ....

Reminder

Name ....

Remember to ....

....

....

Signed ....

Good Thinking

Well done for your thinking skills

Name .... Date ....

We are pleased with you!
For trying hard

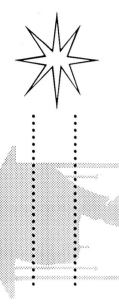

Name ....

signed ....

We are pleased with you

For keeping our Golden Rules

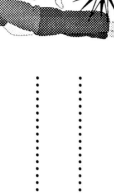

Name ....

signed ....

We are pleased with you!
for working hard

Name ....

signed ....

We are pleased with you!
For making a special effort

Name ....

signed ....

© Jenny Mosley Consultancies, 28A Gloucester Road, Trowbridge, Wiltshire BA14 0AA Tel: 01225 767157 Fax: 01225 755631 Website: www.circle-time.co.uk

Thank you

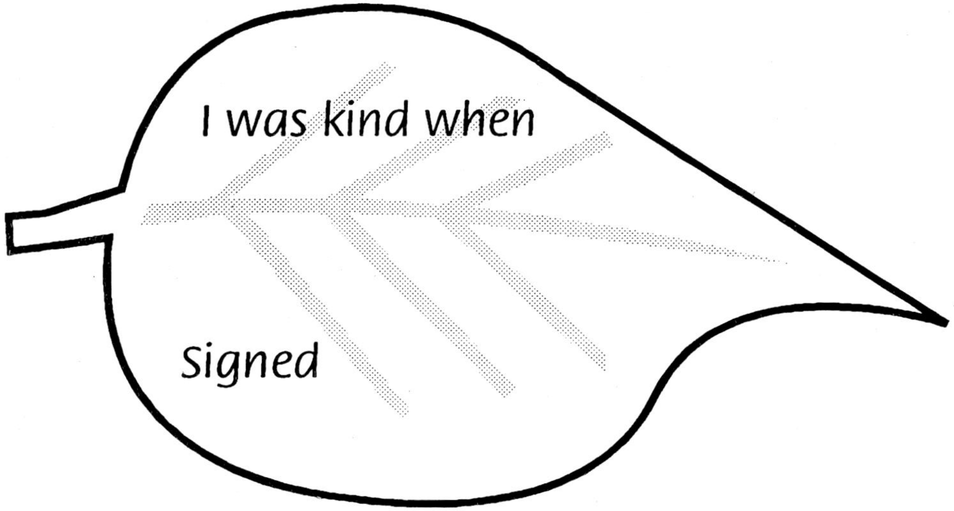

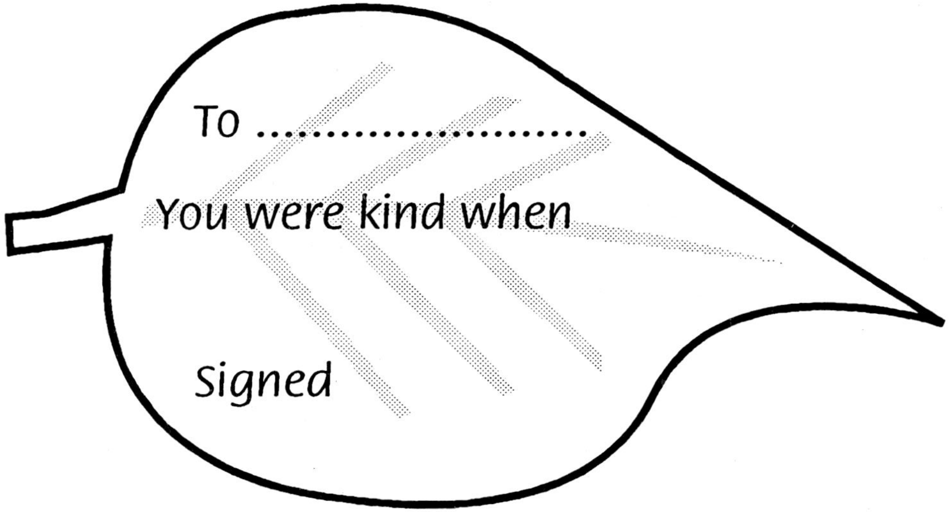

To ....

You were kind when

signed

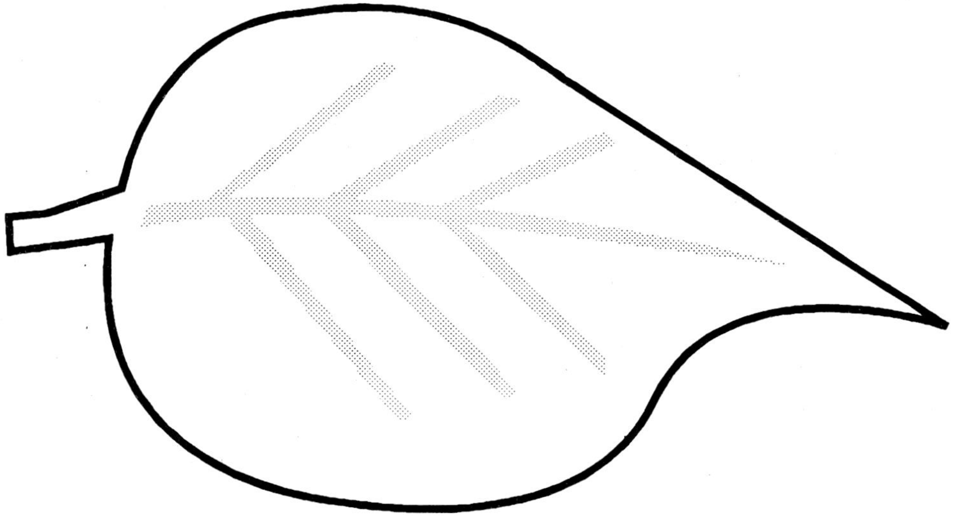

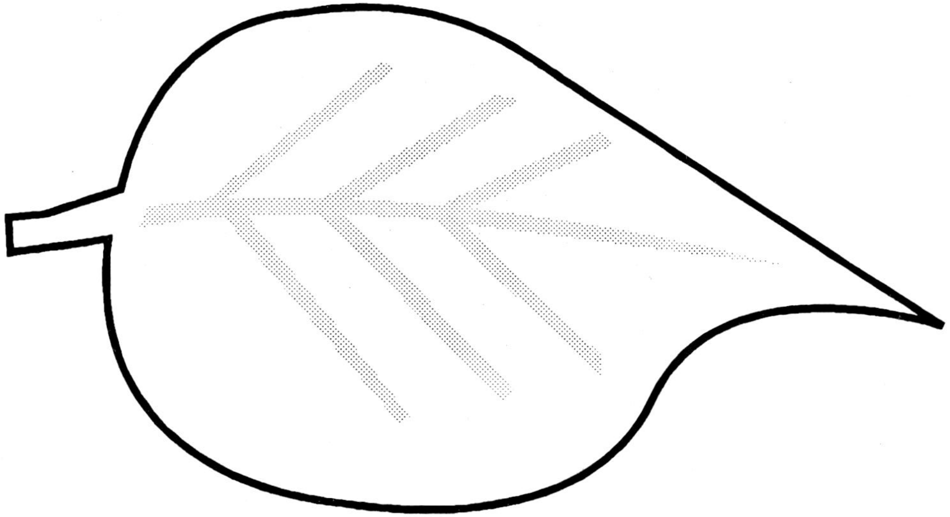

I was kind when

signed

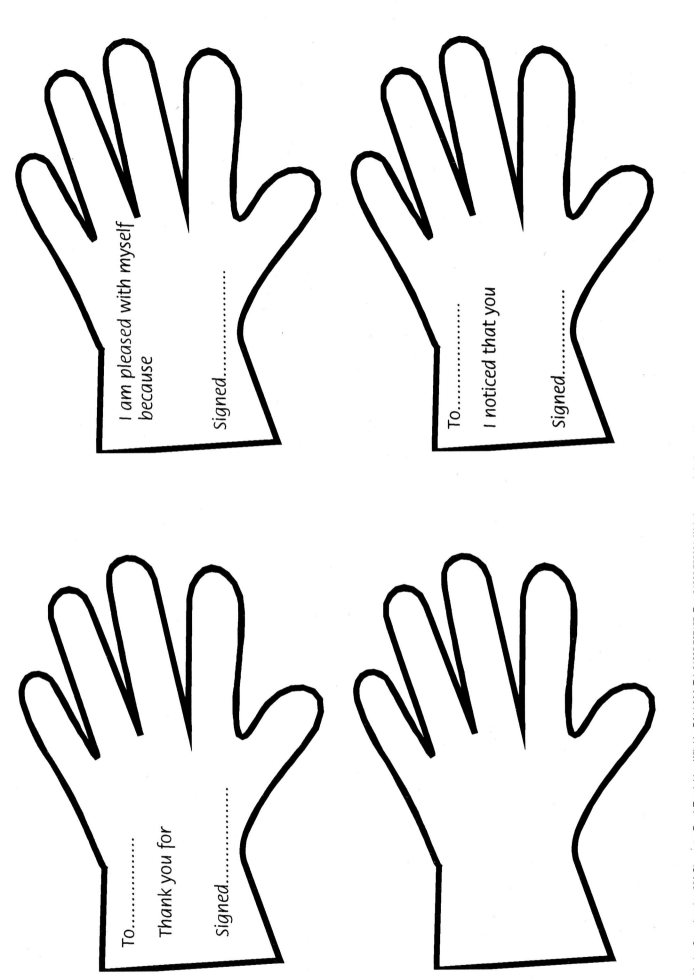

I am pleased with myself
because

signed..............

To..............
I noticed that you

signed..............

To..............
Thank you for

signed..............

All About Me

Name ....   **Date** ....

	Good	Quite Good	Could be better
I listen carefully			
I concentrate on my work			
I carry out a task			
I work well in a group			
I follow instructions			
I speak my thoughts calmly			
I speak out confidently			
I help other children			
I say kind things to others			
I can ask the teacher for help			
I take turns			
I play games happily with others			
I tell others my feelings			
I have stood up for myself			

© Jenny Mosley Consultancies, 28A Gloucester Road, Trowbridge, Wiltshire BA14 0AA Tel: 01225 767157 Fax: 01225 755631 Website: www.circle-time.co.uk

Name ....   Date ....

Anything I like	Anything I don't like

Name ....   Date ....

I am good at	I would like to be better at

I am Special Sheet

Name

My favourite colour is	
My favourite food is	
My favourite activity at home is	
My favourite TV programme is	
My favourite animal is	
I am good at	
This is my shield	

Feelings Colour Chart

Feelings I like

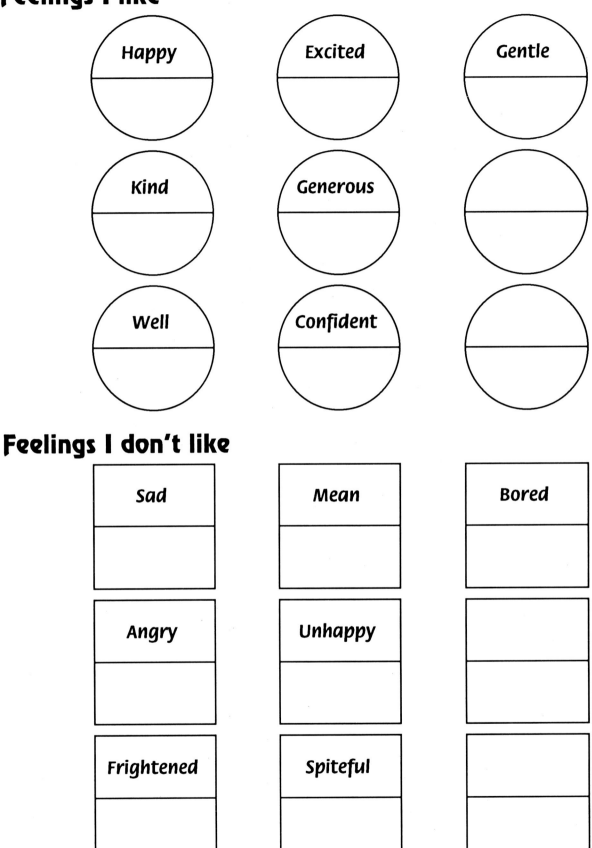

Happy	Excited	Gentle
Kind	Generous	
Well	Confident	

Feelings I don't like

Sad	Mean	Bored
Angry	Unhappy	
Frightened	Spiteful	

Colour in the other half of each feeling with
the colour this feeling suggests to you.

Name.............................

Colour in the balloons and write something you like
or something you are good at in each one

Family Tree

Instructions for Target Sheets

Flower Target Sheet

Each day the target is achieved the child is given a leaf to colour in and stick on the stem. After four leaves (or whatever is the agreed number) the child is given a flower to colour and stick on. (2 pages)

Dog Target Sheet

Each day the target is achieved the child is given a body part to colour and stick onto the body. Finally, the food bowl. (2 pages)

Spaceman Target Sheet

Each day the target is achieved the child is given a part of the spaceman to colour and stick onto the body. (2 pages)

Butterfly Target Sheet

Each day the target is achieved the child is given a part of the caterpillar and then a butterfly to colour in and stick on the leaf. (2 pages)

Cake Target Sheet

Each day the target is achieved the child colours in a layer of the cake and finally the candle on the top. (1 page)

Playtime Target Sheet

each day the target is achieved the child colours in another square on the hopscotch grid. (1 page)

Flower Target Sheet

Name ....

Date ....

Target ....

....

Flower 2

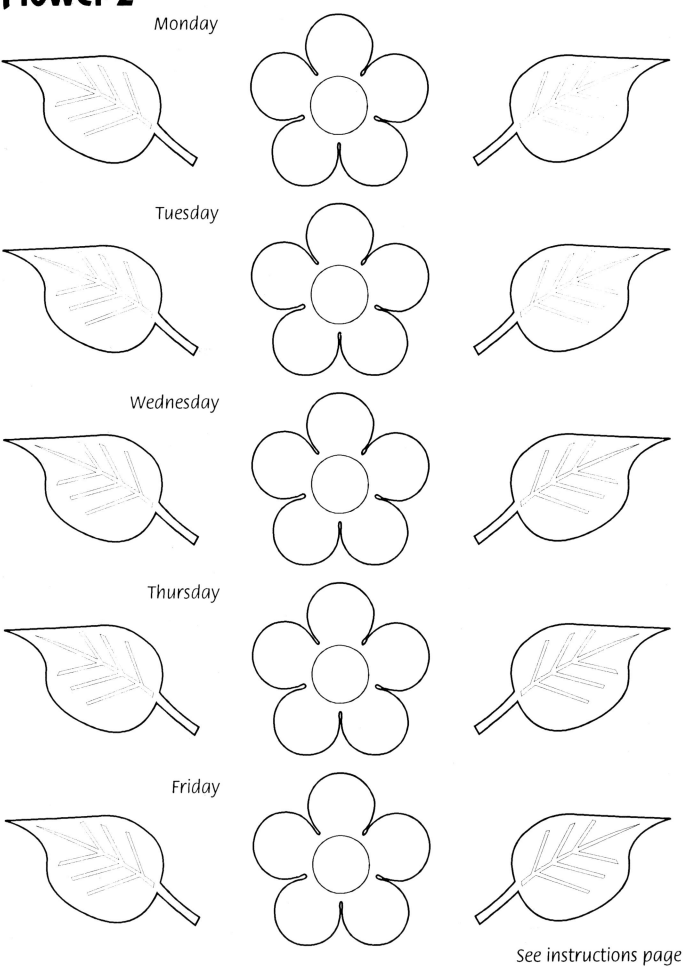

Monday

Tuesday

Wednesday

Thursday

Friday

See instructions page

Dog Target Sheet

Name ....

Date ....

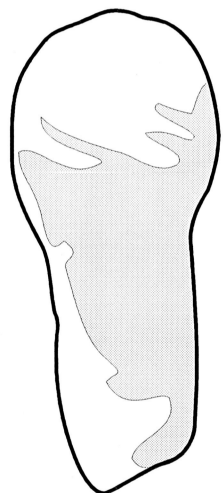

Target ....

Dog 2

Monday

Thursday

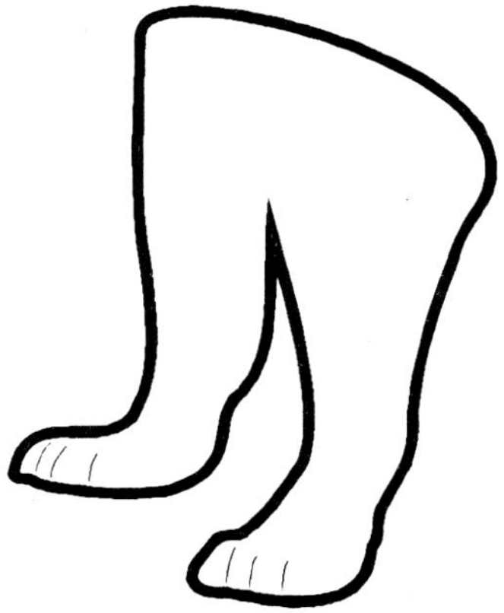

Wednesday

Tuesday

Friday

Good Dog

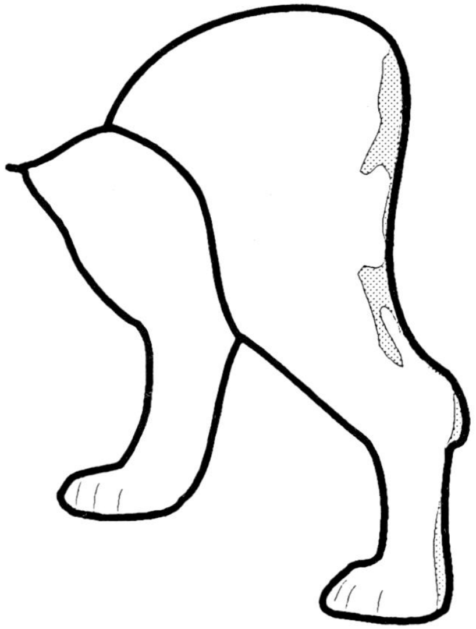

See instruction page

© Jenny Mosley Consultancies, 28A Gloucester Road, Trowbridge, Wiltshire BA14 0AA Tel: 01225 767157 Fax: 01225 755631 Website: www.circle-time.co.uk

Spaceman Target Sheet

Name ....

Date ....

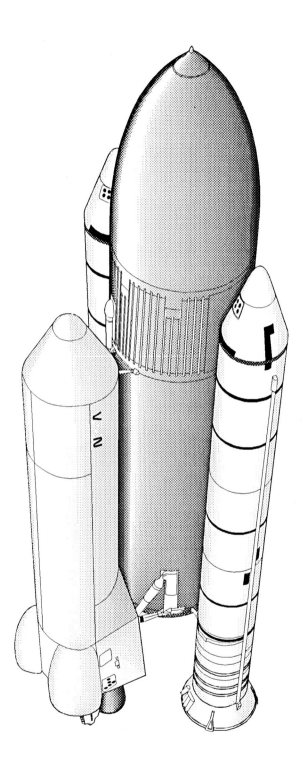

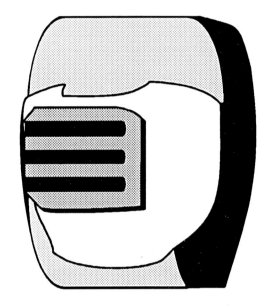

Target ....

© Jenny Mosley Consultancies, 28A Gloucester Road, Trowbridge, Wiltshire BA14 0AA Tel: 01225 767157 Fax: 01225 755631 Website: www.circle-time.co.uk

Spaceman 2

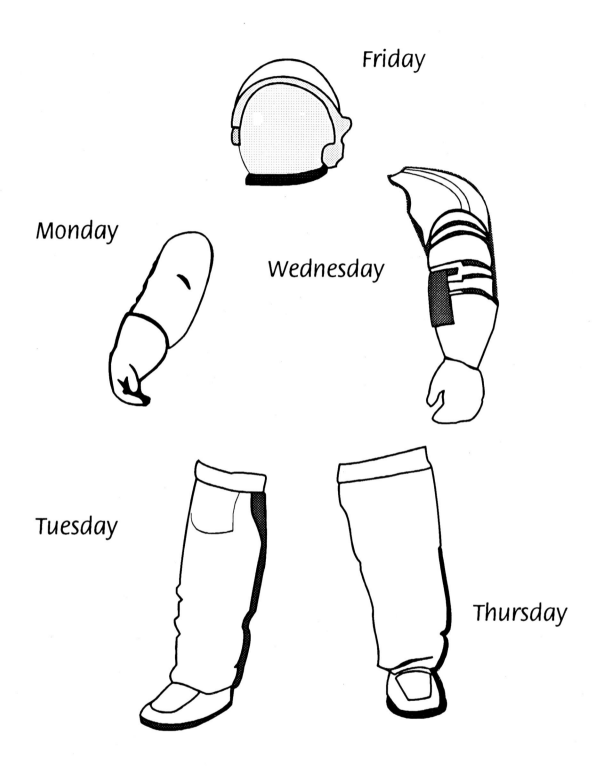

Friday

Monday

Wednesday

Tuesday

Thursday

See instruction page

Butterfly Target Sheet

Name ....

Date ....

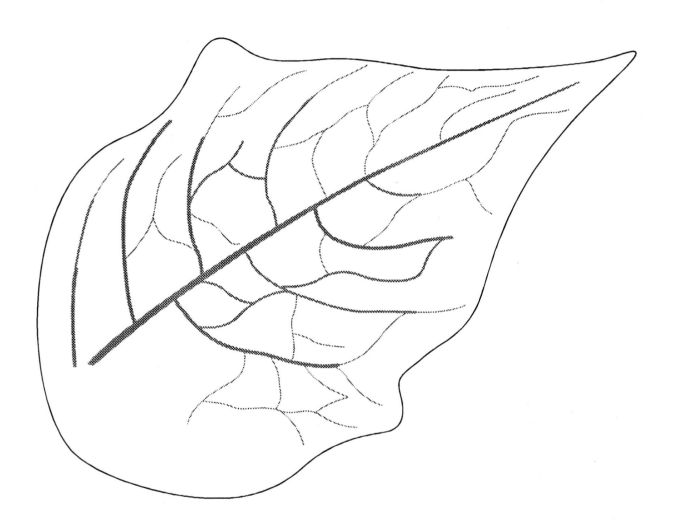

Target ....

Butterfly 2

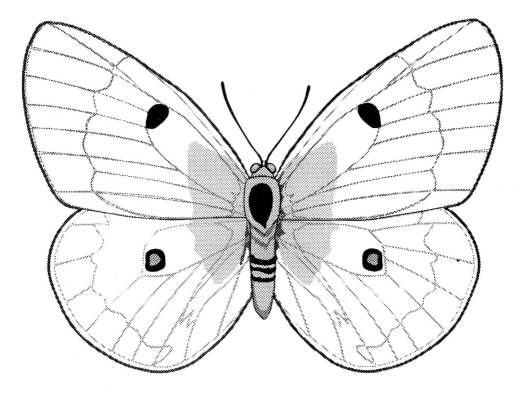

Friday

Monday

Wednesday

Tuesday

Thursday

See instructions page

Cake Target Sheet

Name ....

Date ....

Target ....

....

Playtime Target Chart

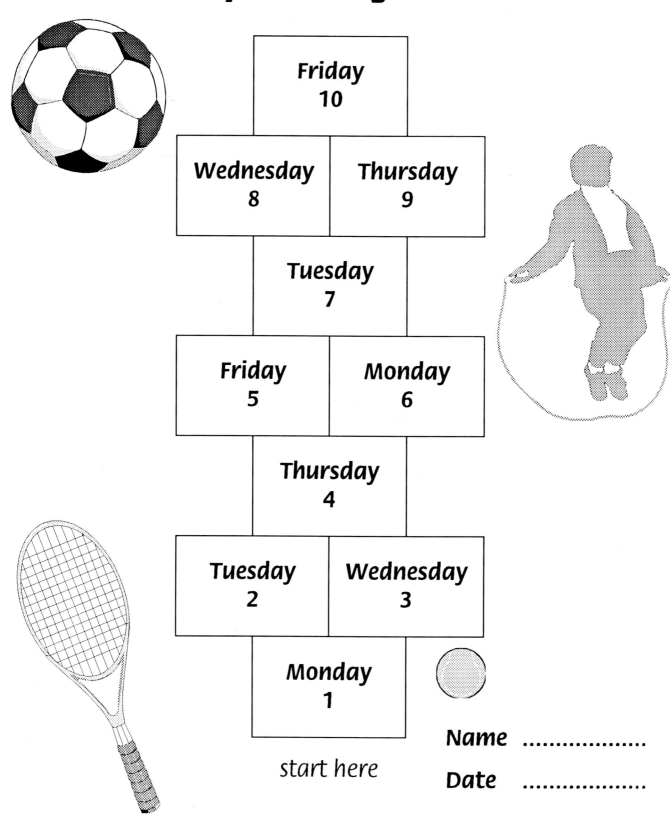

Friday
10

Wednesday
8

Thursday
9

Tuesday
7

Friday
5

Monday
6

Thursday
4

Tuesday
2

Wednesday
3

Monday
1

start here

Name ....

Date ....

Colour in each day that you keep to the Golden Rules.

Well Done

Target Diary

Name ....

Date ....

Monday	Tuesday
My comment	My comment
Teacher's comment	Teacher's comment
Wednesday	**Thursday**
My comment	My comment
Teacher's comment	Teacher's comment
Friday	**Next Plan**
My comment	
Teacher's comment	

Target ....

....

Instructions for Tiny Achievable Tickable Targets (T.A.T.T.'s)

Children beyond the normal motivational procedures such as your incentive and Golden Time systems will need to move onto the T.A.T.T.'s strategy. This involves letting go of the idea that this child can keep to the Golden Rules all the time. You need to negotiate with him/her specific times (using sand timers) where the child keeps the Golden Rules for short periods. If the child reaches this target he/she will have a star/dot put into the appropriate box. You will agree tiny, easy targets at first which can be made more challenging as each is reached. The secret of success lies in the agreed privilege which will accompany reaching the target. It is best when the child has a self-esteem reward, e.g. helping in another class/helping the caretaker. It is also best if you choose a different child from the class to accompany him/her each day as this encourages the others to support the child. Sometimes the most appropriate reward is a class certificate signed by all the children (see class/team honours).

© Jenny Mosley Consultancies, 28A Gloucester Road, Trowbridge, Wiltshire BA14 0AA Tel: 01225 767157 Fax: 01225 755631 Website: www.circle-time.co.uk

Tiny Achievable Tickable Target

	Before play	Playtime	After play	Lunchtime	Afternoon
Monday					
Tuesday					
Wednesday					
Thursday					
Friday					

My target is to get_____stickers each day. If I achieve my target

I can_____

Signed Pupil   ....

Signed Teacher   ....

Tiny Achievable Tickable Target

	Before play	Playtime	After play	Lunchtime	Afternoon
Monday					
Tuesday					
Wednesday					
Thursday					
Friday					

My target is to get_____stickers each day. If I achieve my target

I can_____

Signed Pupil   ....

Signed Teacher   ....

43

© Jenny Mosley Consultancies, 28A Gloucester Road, Trowbridge, Wiltshire BA14 0AA Tel: 01225 767157 Fax: 01225 755631 Website: www.circle-time.co.uk

Class Team Honours

We are really pleased to award

....

a class team honours for ....

....

Signed

44

© Jenny Mosley Consultancies, 28A Gloucester Road, Trowbridge, Wiltshire BA14 0AA Tel: 01225 767157 Fax: 01225 755631 Website: www.circle-time.co.uk

Instructions for Using the Achievement Ladder

By each rung of the ladder, the teacher writes in the achievement agreed with the child, which becomes progressively more demanding for each rung.

Examples

Neat presentation of work could begin with the child writing his name neatly at the bottom rung, progressing through sentences and paragraphs to producing a page of neat work at the top rung.

Working hard in class could begin with two five minute timed periods and progress to a half hour or more.

A reward, which correspondingly becomes greater, is written on the opposite side of the ladder.

Examples

Responsibilities, such as giving out/collecting equipment.

Privileges such as being first in line for lunch, playtime, etc..

Special privilege such as use of certain equipment, opportunity to choose game, etc..

It's a good idea to allow the child to choose the final reward (within reason) as a real incentive to reach the top of the ladder.

The child can choose a figure to climb the ladder and as he reaches each achievement, the figure is moved up one rung. Figures can be fixed to ladder using 'blu-tak'.

© Jenny Mosley Consultancies, 28A Gloucester Road, Trowbridge, Wiltshire BA14 0AA Tel: 01225 767157 Fax: 01225 755631 Website: www.circle-time.co.uk

Well 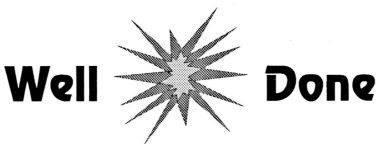 Done

Achievement

Reward

. . . .

. . . .

. . . .

. . . .

. . . .

. . . .

. . . .

. . . .

. . . .

. . . .

. . . .

Achievement Ladder   Name . . . .

46

Figures for Achievement Ladder

See instructions page

47

Achievement Record

Name						

© Jenny Mosley Consultancies, 28A Gloucester Road, Trowbridge, Wiltshire BA14 0AA Tel: 01225 767157 Fax: 01225 755631 Website: www.circle-time.co.uk

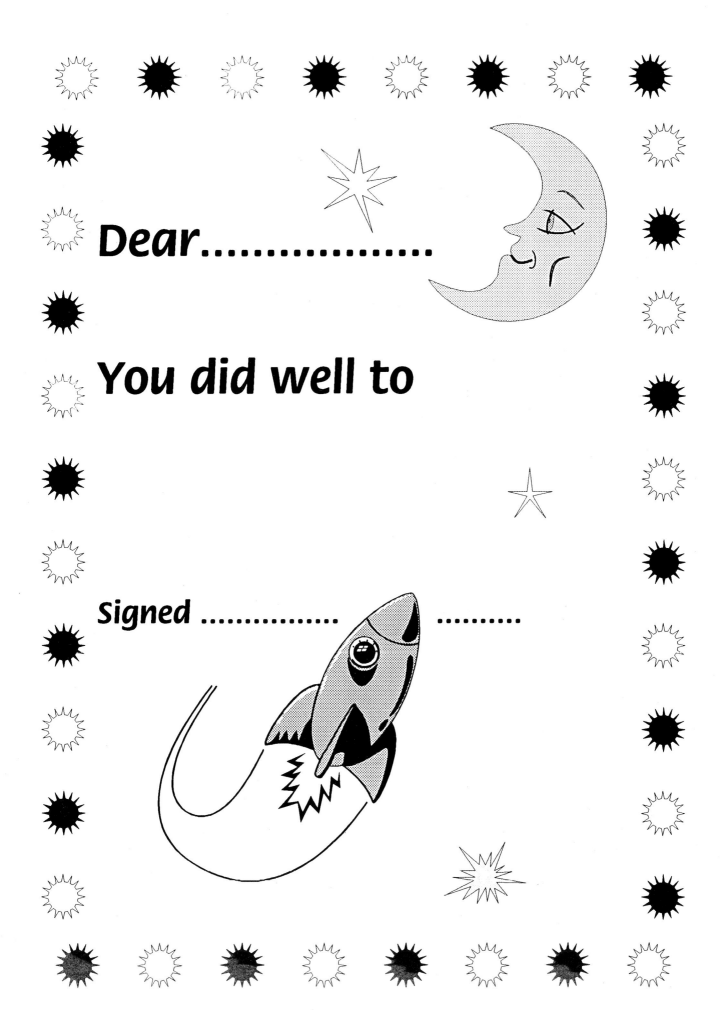

Dear.................

You did well to

Signed ....

TOP SECRET

I just wanted to tell you quietly

Signed......................

Golden Rules

Do....	Don't....
be gentle	hurt anyone
be kind and helpful	hurt people's feelings
be honest	cover up the truth
work hard	waste time
look after property	waste or damage things
listen to people	interrupt

I agree to support the Golden Rules...Parent.